D0573790

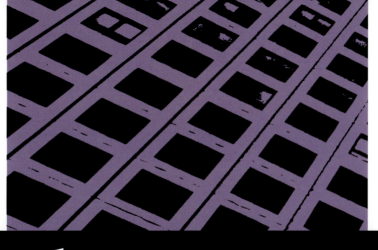

Can You Guess What I Am?
On the Street

J.P. Percy

A⁺

Smart Apple Media

How to use this book

This book combines the fun of a guessing game with some simple information about familiar sights on the street.

Start by guessing
- Carefully study the picture on the right-hand page.
- Decide what you think it might be, using both the picture and the clue.
- Turn the page and find out if you are right.

Don't stop there
- Read the extra information about the animal or object on the following page.
- Turn the page back—did you miss some interesting details?

Enjoy guessing and learning
- Don't worry if you guess wrong— everyone does sometimes.
- Your guessing will get better the more you learn.

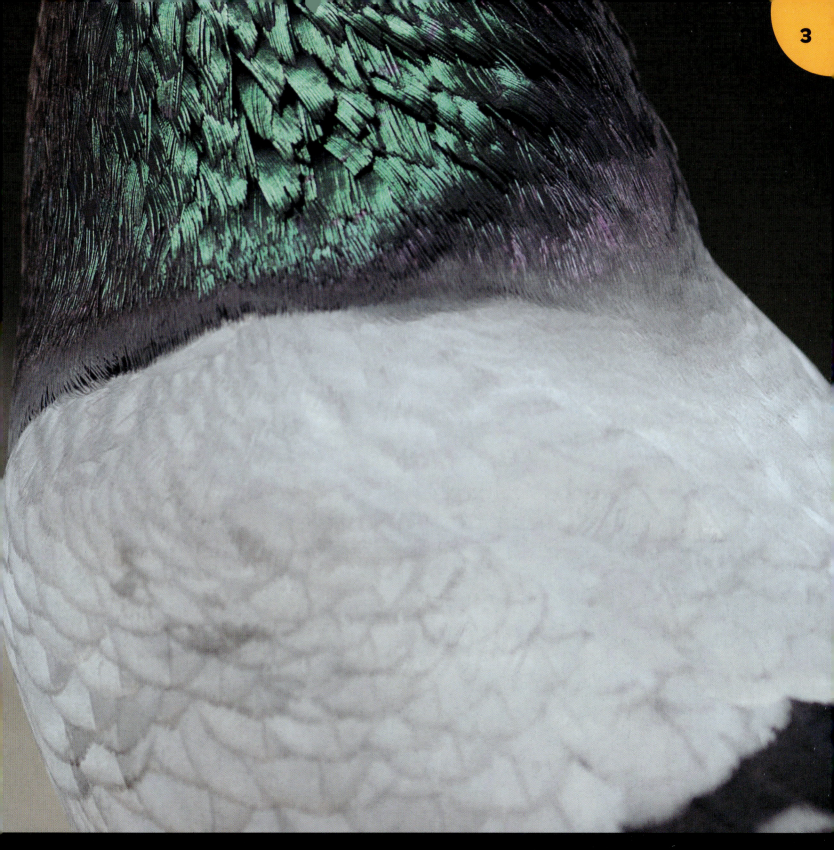

I eat crumbs and I have feathers. Can you guess what I am?

I am a Pigeon!

Many types of pigeons live in towns and cities. In some places, there are so many pigeons that people use birds of prey—such as hawks—to scare the pigeons away.

I go up when it is wet. Can you guess what I am?

I am an umbrella!

The first umbrellas were called parasols. They were used to protect people from the sun. Today, we also use umbrellas to keep us dry when it is raining.

I tell you when to stop or go. Can you guess what I am?

I am a traffic light!

Traffic lights have red, yellow, and green lights. They tell the traffic when to stop and go. Traffic lights help cars and trucks to drive safely in the street.

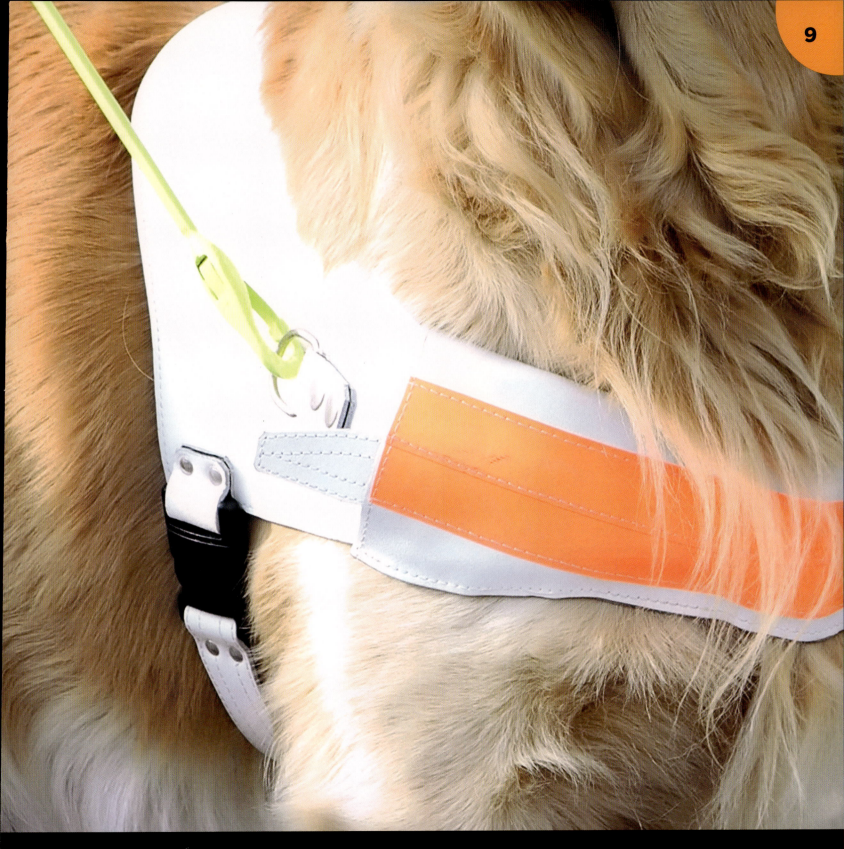

I have four paws and I help my owner. Can you guess what I am?

I am a guide dog!

Guide dogs help people who are blind. They are trained to look out for danger and keep their owners safe on the street.

Riding me on the street is a lot of fun. Can you guess what I am?

I am a bicycle!

Bicycles are a fun way to get around. The harder you push the pedals the faster you can go.

I turn on at night and turn off in the day. Can you guess what I am?

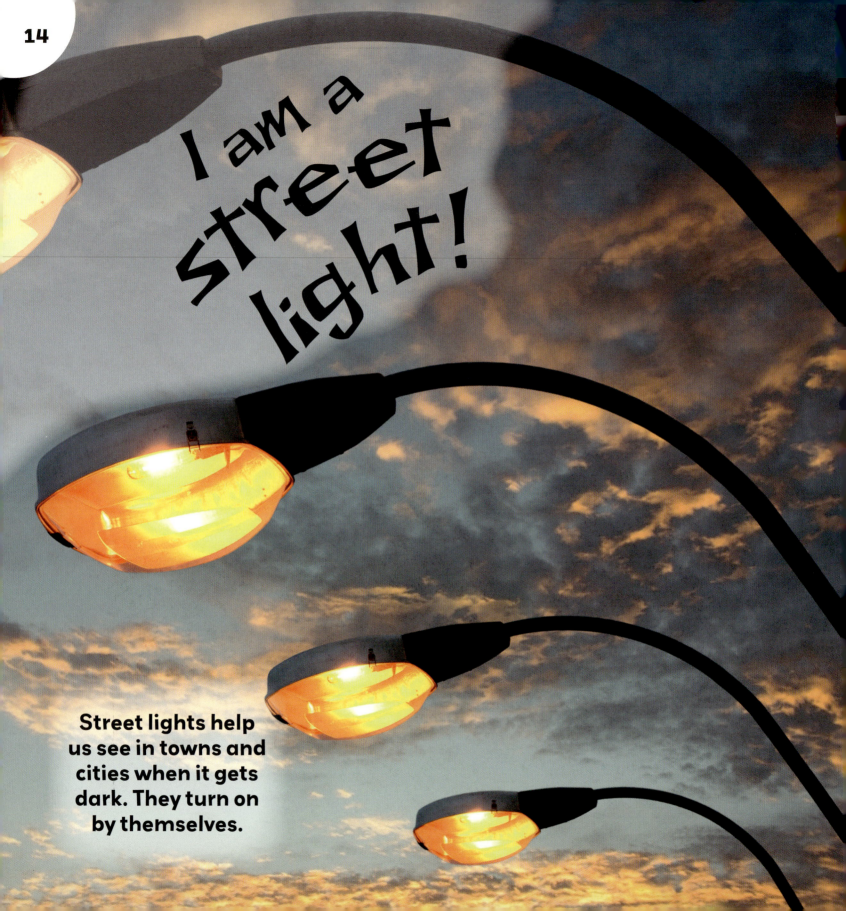

I am a street light!

Street lights help us see in towns and cities when it gets dark. They turn on by themselves.

I have lots of exciting things you can buy. Can you guess what I am?

I am a farmer's market!

The farmer's market is a good place to buy lots of fresh fruit and vegetables. It is a very busy place. The market traders have a variety of foods and crafts for sale.

I move heavy things from place to place. Can you guess what I am?

I am a truck!

Today we use trucks to move big things around. A hundred years ago, we used horses and carts to do the same jobs.

I am noisy and full of people. Can you guess what I am?

I am a parade!

Steet parades are fun ways to celebrate. People dress up in colorful costumes, play music, and sing and dance along the street.

Now try this...

Think it!

The next time you are on the street, imagine you are a guide dog. What does a guide dog need to stay away from to keep its owner safe? Talk about what is dangerous in the street. What can you do to stay safe?

Draw it!

Draw a picture of your favorite vehicle. It could be a car, a truck, or a bus. Draw yourself in the driver's seat of your vehicle or glue a small photograph of yourself behind the wheel.

Write it!

Farmer's markets have lots of things to buy. Some stalls sell fruit or vegetables, and some sell meat or fish. Think of a meal that you enjoy eating. Write a shopping list of ingredients that you could buy from the market.

Published by Smart Apple Media, an imprint of Black Rabbit Books
P.O. Box 3263, Mankato, Minnesota 56002
www.blackrabbitbooks.com

Published by arrangement with the Watts Publishing Group LTD, London.

Library of Congress Cataloging-in-Publication Data
Percy, J.P.
 On the street / J.P. Percy.
    p. cm. — (Can you guess what I am?)
 Summary: "All objects are commonly seen in the street. Use the hint to help guess what is in the close-up photograph. Turn the page to see if you are right and to learn more about the object! "—Provided by publisher.
 ISBN 978-1-59920-894-7 (library binding)
 1. Picture puzzles—Juvenile literature. I. Title.
 GV1507.P47 P473 2013
 793.73—dc23
                          2012033092

Series editor: Amy Stephenson
Art director: Peter Scoulding

Printed in the United States of America at North Mankato, Minnesota
PO1586
2-2013

9 8 7 6 5 4 3 2 1